W9-BRC-641

hot
toddies

hot toddies

Warming winter drinks for chilly days

RYLAND
PETERS
& SMALL

LONDON NEW YORK

Senior Designer Sonya Nathoo
Senior Commissioning Editor Julia Charles
Head of Production Patricia Harrington
Art Director Leslie Harrington
Publishing Director Alison Starling

Indexer Hilary Bird

First published in the United Kingdom in 2011
by Ryland Peters & Small
20–21 Jockey's Fields
London WC1R 4BW
and in the United States
by Ryland Peters & Small, Inc.
519 Broadway, 5th Floor
New York, NY10012

www.rylandpeters.com

The recipes in this book have been published
previously by Ryland Peters & Small.

10 9 8 7 6 5 4 3 2 1

Text © Fiona Beckett, Maxine Clark,
Linda Collister, Tonia George,
Louise Pickford, Ben Reed, Fran Warde
and Ryland Peters & Small 2011

Design and photographs
© Ryland Peters & Small 2011

ISBN: 978 1 84975 151 3

A CIP record for this book is available from the
British Library.

US Library of Congress cataloging-in-publication
data has been applied for

Printed in China

Notes
• All spoon measurements are level unless
otherwise stated.

• All eggs are medium, unless otherwise specified.
It is generally recommended that free-range eggs
be used. Drinks containing raw or partially cooked
egg should not be served to the very young, very
old, anyone with a compromised immune system,
or pregnant women.

• When using slices of citrus fruit such as lemons
or oranges in a drink, try to find organic, unwaxed
fruits and wash well before using. If you can only
find treated fruit, scrub well in warm soapy water
and rinse before using.

contents

some like it hot...

What could be more welcome and comforting than a warming drink on a bitterly cold day? Whilst both tea and coffee in all their various forms are the most widely consumed hot drinks, there is a huge variety of other beverages we like to prepare and serve hot – many of them alcoholic, such as the whiskey toddies, mulled wines, buttered rums, liqueur coffees and spice-infused milk drinks you will discover here. These delicious recipes are guaranteed to not only warm you up quickly, but to stimulate mind, body or soul – and often all three at once!

The benefits of consuming hot drinks are many, yet for most people their greatest appeal is the pleasure derived not only from the drinking, but often from the process of gently warming and stirring various aromatic combinations. This is especially true of those drinks that are enjoyed less regularly, say at Christmastime or other holiday occasions, when many of these brews come into their own and preparing them can become an essential part of a family's festive traditions.

With wonderful recipes to choose from in this book, you should find something delicious to drink on any occasion throughout the winter. Whether you are looking for a party punch for a crowd, or something to help you wind down in front of a roaring fire at the end of a the day, you are sure to find it here.

toddies & cocktails

hot toddy

5 cloves
2 lemon slices
50 ml/2 oz whiskey
25 ml/1 oz freshly squeezed lemon juice
2 teaspoons clear honey or sugar syrup, to taste
80 ml/$\frac{1}{3}$ cup just-boiled water
1 cinnamon stick, to serve (optional)

Serves 1

The Hot Toddy, with its warming blend of spices and sweet honey aroma, is the perfect comforter and will soothe any aches, pains or winter snuffles. It's also a great life-saver for cold afternoons spent outside watching sport. Next time you have need to pack a thermos flask of coffee, think again and mix up a batch of this recipe, then see how popular you are!

Skewer the cloves into the lemon slices and put them in a heatproof glass.

Add the whiskey, lemon juice and honey or sugar syrup to taste. Top up with boiling water and add a cinnamon stick to serve, if using. Serve immediately.

hot tea toddy

A variation of the classic Hot Toddy (see page 9), this comforting drink is especially good if you think you are coming down with a cold. Use decaffeinated tea for a relaxing bedtime drink.

500 ml/2 cups freshly brewed hot tea

4 tablespoons cognac

4 tablespoons dark rum

4 thin strips of lemon zest

12 cloves

2–3 teaspoons clear honey, to taste

2 lemon slices, to serve

2 cinnamon sticks, to serve (optional)

Serves 2

Put the tea, cognac, rum, lemon zest, cloves and honey in a saucepan and gently heat for 5 minutes without boiling.

Remove the pan from the heat, let the mixture infuse for 5 minutes. Strain into 2 cups or heatproof glasses and serve immediately with a slice of lemon in each one and a cinnamon stick, if liked.

hot buttered rum

two 30-ml/1 oz shots dark rum

4 cloves

2 lemon slices

2 teaspoons unrefined caster/superfine sugar

250 ml/1 cup just-boiled water

30 g/2 tablespoons unsalted butter

2 cinnamon sticks

Serves 2

This is a simple mulled rum drink with the curious addition of butter, which gives it some extra richness. It's the perfect indulgence for a chilly winter evening.

Put a shot of rum into each of 2 heatproof glasses and add the cloves, lemon slices and sugar.

Top up with boiling water and add half the butter to each drink. Put a cinnamon stick in each one and use to stir the butter as it melts. Serve immediately.

blue blazer

1 sugar cube
50 ml/2 oz just-boiled water
50 ml/2 oz whiskey
freshly grated nutmeg,
to serve

Serves 1

A spectacular drink to serve, but one that is best practised
in the safe confines of the kitchen before trying it in front of
an audience. Cocktails created using a naked flame are best
kept for the start of the evening, for obvious reasons!

Warm 2 small metal tankards. In one, dissolve the sugar cube in
the boiling water. Pour the whiskey into the other. Set the whiskey
alight using an extra-long match or a taper to keep your hands well
away from the flame.

As it burns, pour the liquid into the first tankard and back, from one
to another, creating a continuous stream of fire. Once the flame has
died down, pour the mixture into a warmed old-fashioned glass and
sprinkle with nutmeg to serve.

mulled bloody Mary

This is totally delicious and tastes exactly as you'd imagine a warmed version of the classic brunch drink to taste. It is perfect for a cold winter's morning, especially if you've over-indulged the night before!

1 litre/4 cups tomato juice

1 lemon

1–2 tablespoons Worcestershire sauce, to taste

100–125 ml/^{1}/$_3$–^{1}/$_2$ cup vodka

a pinch of celery salt

sea salt and freshly ground black pepper

Serves 4–6

Put the tomato juice in a saucepan. Cut half the lemon into slices and squeeze the juice from the remaining half into the pan. Add the lemon slices, Worcestershire sauce and some salt and pepper to taste. Bring slowly to the boil and simmer gently, uncovered, for 10 minutes.

Remove the pan from the heat and let cool for about 20 minutes. Stir in the vodka and add celery salt to taste. Serve immediately.

mulls & punches

mulled wine

two 750-ml/3-cup bottles
fruity red wine

2 oranges

8 cloves

3 tablespoons brown sugar

5-cm/2-in piece of fresh ginger,
peeled and chopped

1 cinnamon stick

½ teaspoon freshly grated
nutmeg

Serves 4–6

Fill your house with warming aromas and make your friends' hearts glow with this beautiful spicy drink. If you're making it for a big party, simply add more wine and sugar to the saucepan as the evening wears on.

Pour the red wine into a large saucepan. Stud the oranges with the cloves, then cut each orange into quarters. Add to the pan, together with the sugar, ginger, cinnamon and nutmeg.

Heat the mixture to simmering point and simmer for 8–10 minutes. Ladle into small heatproof glasses or cups to serve.

orange mulled wine

two 750-ml/3-cup bottles
fruity red wine

500 ml/2 cups cold water

1 orange, plus a few orange
slices to serve

a small handful of cloves

thinly pared zest of
$1/2$ a lemon

2 cinnamon sticks

6 cardamom pods,
lightly crushed

a little freshly grated nutmeg
or a small pinch of
ground nutmeg

100 g/$1/2$ cup soft brown sugar

100 ml/$1/3$ cup Grand Marnier,
Cointreau or other
orange-flavoured liqueur

Serves 14–16

If you've never made mulled wine yourself, you should try.
It couldn't be simpler and tastes infinitely better than the
ready-mixed versions. The only thing you have to be careful
about is that the wine doesn't boil.

Pour the wine and water into a large saucepan. Stud the orange
with the cloves and add it to the pan, along with the lemon zest,
spices and sugar. Heat gently until almost boiling. Turn down to the
lowest possible heat so that the liquid barely trembles and simmer
for 30 minutes to let the spices infuse. Add the orange-flavoured
liqueur, then reheat gently.

Strain into a large, warmed bowl and float a few thin slices of
orange on top. Ladle into small heatproof glasses or cups to serve.

Swedish glögg

1 orange

two 750-ml/3-cup bottles dry red wine

one 750-ml/3-cup bottle aquavit or vodka

12 cardamom pods, crushed

8 cloves

3-cm/1$^1/_4$-in piece of fresh ginger, sliced

1 cinnamon stick

250 g/1$^1/_2$ cups sugar

200 g/1$^1/_3$ cup raisins

200 g/1$^1/_4$ cups blanched almonds

Serves 20

'Glögg' is the Scandinavian version of German 'glühwein' or mulled wine. It's ideal for a party but you will need to get it started the day beforehand.

Using a vegetable peeler, remove the zest from the orange in a single curl (do not include any of the bitter white pith). Put all the ingredients, except the almonds, in a large stainless-steel or enamel saucepan and set aside overnight (at least 12 hours).

Just before serving, heat to just below boiling point. (Do not let the liquid boil or the alcohol will be burned off.) Remove from the heat and stir in the almonds.

Serve in glass punch cups or tea glasses, with small spoons so that the softened almonds and raisins can be scooped out and eaten.

mulled cider

one 500-ml/2-cup bottle
traditional dry/hard cider

125 ml/½ cup Calvados (French
apple brandy) or brandy

750 ml/3 cups cloudy
unsweetened apple juice

75 g/⅓ cup soft brown sugar

a thinly pared strip of
lemon zest

2 cinnamon sticks

8 cloves

6 even-sized slices of dried
apple, halved

10–12 cinnamon sticks,
to serve (optional)

Serves 10–12

**This makes such a delicious alternative to mulled wine that
you may find that you like it even better!**

Put the cider, Calvados and apple juice in a large saucepan. Add
the sugar, lemon zest, cinnamon sticks and cloves and heat very
gently until the sugar has dissolved. Heat until almost boiling, then
turn off the heat, add the halved, dried apple slices and leave the
mixture for 30 minutes for the flavours to infuse.

Reheat, taking care not to let it boil. Ladle into small heatproof
glasses or cups to serve with a slice of the dried apple and
a cinnamon stick to each (if using).

Portuguese mulled port

2 oranges
500 ml/2 cups water
50 g/¼ cup brown sugar
10 cloves, lightly crushed
6 allspice berries, crushed
1 cinnamon stick, crushed
¼ teaspoon freshly grated nutmeg
one 750-ml/3-cup bottle of ruby port

Serves 12

Similar to mulled wine but made using port, this is an elegant spiced punch, perfect for a winter cocktail party. It is fairly potent so serve it in small demitasse cups as an aperitif.

Peel and slice 1 orange and squeeze the juice from the second orange. Put the slices and juice in a saucepan and add the water, sugar, cloves, allspice, cinnamon stick and nutmeg. Bring slowly to the boil, stirring until the sugar is dissolved.

Simmer gently for 10 minutes. Stir in the port and heat gently, without boiling, for a further 2–3 minutes. Strain and pour into small cups or heatproof glasses to serve.

one 500-ml/2-cup bottle
dry/hard cider
2 lemon slices
1 apple, cored and thinly sliced
1 cinnamon stick, crushed
3 cloves
2 tablespoons soft light
brown sugar
65 ml/¼ cup dark rum

Serves 4–6

hot rum & cider punch

What's not to love about this warming drink with its slices of apple infused with the flavours of the cider, rum and spices? It would make a great drink for a Halloween party. If you want to serve a family–friendly, non-alcoholic version, simply replace the cider with soft apple juice and omit the rum.

Put the cider, lemon slices, apple slices, cinnamon, cloves, sugar and rum in a large saucepan and heat the mixture gently until it just reaches boiling point.

Simmer very gently for 10 minutes, then remove from the heat and let infuse for 10 minutes. Ladle into small heatproof glasses or cups to serve.

nogs &
creamy drinks

egg nog

3 very fresh large eggs*

75 g/generous ⅓ cup caster/superfine sugar

100 ml/⅓ cup bourbon

100 ml/⅓ cup spiced rum

570 ml/2⅓ cups milk

275 ml/1 cup plus 2 tablespoons whipping cream

freshly grated nutmeg, to serve

Serves 6–8

*see note on page 4 about serving partially cooked eggs

Once you've tasted this deliciously light, foamy punch, I suspect you'll want to make it every year. This version is adapted from a recipe in top American bartender Dale Degroff's fabulous book *The Craft of the Cocktail*.

Separate the egg yolks carefully from the whites and put them in separate large bowls. Beat the egg yolks with a hand-held electric whisk, gradually adding 50 g/¼ cup of the sugar, until they turn light in colour and moussey in texture. Beat in the bourbon and spiced rum, then stir in the milk and cream.

Clean and dry the whisk thoroughly, then whisk the egg whites until beginning to stiffen. Add the remaining sugar and whisk again until they form soft peaks. Fold the whites into the egg nog mixture and grate over a little nutmeg. The egg nog can be served cold or gently heated in a large saucepan until just warm, as preferred. Ladle into small glasses or cups to serve.

egg-nog latte

500 ml/2 cups milk

1 vanilla bean, split

2 very fresh eggs*

2–3 tablespoons caster/superfine sugar, to taste

1/2 teaspoon ground cinnamon

a pinch of freshly grated nutmeg

2 tablespoons dark rum

250 ml/1 cup freshly brewed hot coffee

Serves 6–8

*see note on page 4 about serving partially cooked eggs

This warming, festive drink with a hint of coffee makes a lovely alternative to the more traditional egg nog (see page 31). For a non-alcoholic version, simply omit the rum.

Put the milk and vanilla bean in a large saucepan and heat gently, until the milk just reaches boiling point.

Meanwhile, put the eggs, sugar and spices in a bowl and whisk until frothy. Remove the vanilla bean, stir the milk into the egg mixture, then return it to the pan. Heat gently for 2–3 minutes, stirring with a wooden spoon, until the mixture thickens slightly.

Remove from the heat and stir in the rum and coffee. Pour into heatproof glasses and serve immediately.

spiced hot chocolate

600 ml/2½ cups milk

75 g/3 oz dark chocolate (at least 70% cocoa solids), chopped

2 star anise

finely grated zest of ½ an orange

1 tablespoon orange-blossom or acacia honey

75 ml/⅓ cup spiced dark rum

50 ml/¼ cup Grand Marnier or other orange-flavoured liqueur

cinnamon sticks and whipped cream, to serve (optional)

Serves 2

This is an instant mood lifter – make this drink when you are feeling a bit dejected and it cannot fail to lift your spirits. Watch out though – it is quite potent!

Put the milk, chocolate, star anise, orange zest and honey in a saucepan and heat gently, stirring constantly, until the chocolate has melted.

Remove the star anise and discard. Add the rum and Grand Marnier and liquidize in a blender until completely smooth and frothy. Pour into warmed heatproof glasses. Add a cinnamon stick, if using, and top with whipped cream if desired. Serve immediately.

honey rum baba

500 ml/2 cups milk
2 cinnamon sticks, lightly crushed
2 teaspoons clear honey
60 ml/¼ cup white rum
cinnamon sugar, to dust

Serves 2

This is a delicately spiced milk drink infused with a hint of honey and a little rum for a grown-up treat.

Put the milk and cinnamon sticks in a saucepan and heat gently until the mixture just reaches boiling point. Remove from the heat and strain well.

Add 1 teaspoon honey to each serving cup and pour in the cinnamon-infused milk. Add the rum and stir in. Dust with a little cinnamon sugar and serve immediately.

polar bear

250 ml/1 cup milk

250 ml/1 cup double/ heavy cream

75 g/3 oz good-quality white chocolate, grated, plus extra to serve

80 ml/⅓ cup Kahlúa or other coffee-flavoured liqueur

125 ml/½ cup whipping cream

white or dark chocolate-coated coffee beans, to serve

Serves 2

This delicious drink looks innocent enough in a glass, but don't be deceived by looks – this creamy cocktail packs a punch! It's very rich and filling so it could easily be served as an alternative to dessert.

Put the milk and cream in a saucepan and heat gently until it just reaches boiling point. Remove the pan from the heat and stir in the chocolate until melted, then add the Kahlúa. Divide between 2 heatproof glasses or cups.

Whip the cream until thick, then spoon it over the drinks. Sprinkle with grated white chocolate and top with a few chocolate-coated coffee beans to serve.

cinnamon mocha

50 g/2 oz dark chocolate, broken into pieces

250 ml/1 cup milk

1 tablespoon sugar

1 cinnamon stick

250 ml/1 cup freshly brewed hot, strong coffee

2 tablespoons brandy (optional)

2 curls of orange zest

cinnamon sticks dipped in melted chocolate, to serve (see recipe introduction)

Serves 2

Dip long cinnamon sticks into melted chocolate, leave to set, then use to stir this special drink.

Put the chocolate, milk, sugar and cinnamon in heavy-based saucepan and heat gently, stirring constantly, until melted and smooth. Bring the mixture to the boil, whisking constantly with a balloon whisk, then remove from the heat and whisk in the coffee and brandy.

Remove the cinnamon stick. Put the curls of orange peel in tall, warmed, heatproof glasses, pour over the hot mixture, add a chocolate-dipped cinnamon stick and serve immediately.

white Christmas

This is a delicious drink full of festive flavours. If you like frothy drinks, then a milk frother is an absolute must. There are various types but basically they are tools that froth milk into a foam stiff enough to be spooned on top of a hot drink.

1 litre/4 cups milk

200 g/7 oz good-quality white chocolate, grated, plus extra to serve

2 orange slices

4 cloves, lightly crushed

2 cinnamon sticks, lightly crushed

a pinch of freshly grated nutmeg

75 ml/⅓ cup Grand Marnier, Cointreau or other orange-flavoured liqueur

125 ml/½ cup whipping cream, whipped

candied orange zest, to serve

Serves 6

Put the milk, chocolate, orange and spices in a saucepan and heat gently, stirring, until it just reaches boiling point. Froth the milk with a milk frother or whisk vigorously with a flat or small round whisk until the mixture is foamy.

Divide between 6 small cups or heatproof glasses and pour in the Grand Marnier. Spoon some whipped cream on top of each one and sprinkle with candied orange zest and grated chocolate to serve.

tipsy coffees

Irish coffee

60 ml/¼ cup Irish whiskey

4 shots freshly brewed hot espresso coffee

20 ml/1 generous tablespoon sugar syrup

250 ml/1 cup double/ heavy cream

6 coffee beans, to serve

Serves 2

The trick to this popular digestif is not to go crazy with the cream. Sweetening the coffee does help the cream sit on top well, but if you don't take sugar it should still work – you'll just need a steadier hand.

Mix the whiskey, coffee and sugar syrup, to taste, in heatproof glasses, making sure the coffee is piping hot.

Slowly layer the cream over the surface of the coffee, using a flat-bottomed barspoon or a teaspoon. Top with three coffee beans and serve immediately.

Caribbean coffee with Malibu & rum

2–4 teaspoons caster/superfine sugar, to taste

2 tablespoons dark rum

2 tablespoons Malibu, or other coconut-flavoured liqueur

250 ml/1 cup freshly brewed hot coffee

80 ml/¹⁄₃ cup whipping cream

Serves 2

This exotic-flavoured coffee is similar to an Irish coffee (see page 45) but full of the tropical flavours of coconut and rum.

Divide the sugar, rum, Malibu and coffee between 2 heatproof glasses and stir well.

Put the cream in a bowl and whisk until foaming. Slowly layer the cream over the surface of each coffee, using a flat-bottomed barspoon or a teaspoon. Serve immediately.

mocha maple coffee

500 ml/2 cups freshly brewed hot coffee

60 ml/¼ cup crème de cacao or chocolate syrup

125 ml/½ cup whipping cream

1 teaspoon pure maple syrup

finely grated dark chocolate, to serve

Serves 2

Coffee and chocolate make perfect partners as this delicious drink proves. The addition of sweet, maple syrup-flavoured cream makes this an indulgent after-dinner drink.

Pour the freshly brewed coffee into 2 heatproof glasses and add half of the crème de cacao or chocolate syrup to each one.

Lightly whisk the cream and maple syrup together until the mixture is foaming and thickened slightly. Slowly layer the cream over the surface of the coffee using a flat-bottomed barspoon or a teaspoon. Sprinkle with grated chocolate and serve immediately.

Catalan coffee punch

250 ml/1 cup white rum

1–2 tablespoons caster/superfine sugar

1 cinnamon stick

2 strips of lemon zest

500 ml/2 cups freshly brewed hot coffee

Serves 6–8

This is a traditional hot coffee and rum drink from the Catalonia region of Spain. It is traditional to use a terracotta cooking vessel for this, but a stainless-steel saucepan will work just as well. Be careful when igniting the rum. Use an extra-long match or a taper to keep your hands well away from the flame.

Put the rum, sugar, cinnamon and lemon zest in a terracotta pot (or other flameproof pan) and carefully ignite the mixture. Let the flame die down completely then slowly pour in the hot coffee.

Divide between heavy-based shot glasses or heatproof demitasse cups and serve immediately.

non-alcoholic warmers

pumpkin latte

400 ml/1²/₃ cups milk

100 g/¹/₂ cup mashed cooked sweet pumpkin or canned pumpkin purée

3 tablespoons brown sugar

¹/₄ teaspoon ground cinnamon

250 ml/1 cup freshly brewed hot coffee

whipped cream and cinnamon sugar, to serve

Serves 3

Perfect served at any Halloween get-together, this thick, richly spiced latte is enriched with sweetened pumpkin. If you can find canned sweetened pumpkin purée, then use this and omit the sugar in the recipe.

Put the milk, pumpkin, sugar (if using) and cinnamon in a saucepan and heat gently, whisking constantly until the mixture just reaches boiling point.

Transfer to 3 cups or heatproof glasses and stir in the coffee. Serve immediately topped with lightly whipped cream and a dusting of cinnamon sugar.

saffron milk

400 ml/1²/₃ cups milk

60 ml/¹/₄ cup sweetened condensed milk

¹/₄ teaspoon saffron threads, plus extra to serve

3 cardamom pods, lightly crushed

Serves 2

Exotic saffron, with its earthy taste, makes this recipe delicious as well as pretty. The condensed milk does make this drink very sweet so, if preferred, reduce the amount used and increase the quantity of milk accordingly.

Put the milk, condensed milk, saffron and cardamom pods in a saucepan and heat gently, stirring constantly, until the mixture just reaches boiling point.

Remove from the heat and let infuse for 5 minutes. Strain the milk into 2 heatproof glasses, sprinkle with a few saffron threads and serve immediately.

Thai coffee

160 ml/²/₃ cup sweetened condensed milk, at room temperature

375 ml/1¹/₂ cups freshly brewed strong, hot coffee

Serves 2

Coffee in Thailand is often served iced but can be served hot too. It is always very sweet as it is served over sweetened condensed milk. You can either stir the coffee and milk together or drink the hot coffee first and then enjoy the warm milk underneath.

Divide the condensed milk between 2 heatproof glasses then very carefully pour in the coffee so that it sits on top of the milk. Stir if you like, then serve immediately.

variation Add a little freshly ground cardamom and ground coriander to your ground coffee before brewing.

Moroccan spiced coffee

1 cinnamon stick, crumbled

seeds from 3 cardamom pods

$\frac{1}{4}$ teaspoon fennel seeds

2 teaspoons toasted
sesame seeds

50 g/2 oz medium-ground
coffee

500 ml/2 cups just-boiled water

milk and sugar, to taste
(optional)

Serves 2–4

This is a lovely aromatic coffee with spices and the unusual
addition of ground toasted sesame seeds – these add a
wonderful nutty flavour to the coffee. This recipe makes
2 large or 4 small cups.

Put the spices and sesame seeds in a spice grinder and grind finely.
Stir into the ground coffee and use this mixture to make coffee
in your preferred method adding milk and/or sugar if you like.

Indian chai masala

This spiced Indian tea has become popular in the West – not surprising as it's a delicious and reviving drink.

¼ teaspoon freshly grated nutmeg

¼ teaspoon finely grated fresh ginger

3 cloves

seeds from 3 cardamom pods

a pinch of ground cinnamon

200 ml/¾ cup water

100 ml/⅓ cup milk

2 teaspoons sugar

1 teaspoon black tea leaves

Serves 2

Mix the spices well. Put the water, milk and sugar in a saucepan. Add the tea and spices. Bring to the boil, reduce the heat and simmer for 2 minutes. Strain into 2 cups and serve immediately.

variation Try altering the spice mixture to suit your own taste. Use ground ginger if making a larger quantity.

index

recipe credits

Louise Pickford
Caribbean coffee with
  Malibu and rum
Catalan coffee punch
Egg-nog latte
Honey rum baba
Hot buttered rum
Hot rum and cider punch
Mocha maple coffee
Moroccan spiced coffee
Mulled bloody Mary
Polar bear
Portuguese mulled port
Pumpkin latte
Saffron milk
Thai coffee
White Christmas

Ben Reed
Blue blazer
Hot toddy
Irish coffee

Tonia George
Hot tea toddy

Maxine Clark
Spiced rum chocolate
Swedish glögg

Fiona Beckett
Egg nog
Mulled cider
Orange mulled wine

Fran Warde
Mulled wine

Hattie Ellis
Indian chai masala

Linda Collister
Cinnamon mocha

photography credits

Martin Brigdale
Pages 10, 38, 40, 60

Peter Cassidy
Pages 5 centre, 6, 11, 20,
24, 25, 28, 30, 35, 37,
55, 56

Tara Fisher
Pages 33, 49

Jonathan Gregson
Pages 26, 41, 42

Richard Jung
Page 12, 59

William Lingwood
Pages 2, 5 above,
5 below, 8, 13, 14, 17,
27, 29, 32, 34, 36, 39,
43, 44, 46, 47, 48, 51,
52, 54, 57, 58

David Montgomery
Page 16

Noel Murphy
Page 23

Steve Painter
Page 50

Debi Treloar
Pages 1, 18, 61

Kate Whitaker
Pages 21, 22

Alan Williams
Page 15